I NEVER WALKED ALONE

ALONE

A POETIC INSPIRATIONAL STORY OF OVERCOMING STRUGGLE

THELMA K. HASKINS

Heather James Miller Media, LLC
c/o Thelma K. Haskins
P.O. Box 952
Locust Grove, VA 22508
heather@heatherjamesmiller.com

Scripture quotations identified KJV are from the Holy Bible, New King James Version
Contributor Credits: Tomi Reed-Smith, Teresa Reed, Theda Harmon, Trudy Otis, Christine Reed, Diamond McCoy, Kelly Norman Ellis, Cheryl Slaughter Ellis and Olivia Kelley Slaughter.

Book design by HJM Media, LLC
Cover Image by Ashley Knedler, Unsplash.com
Interior design by HJM Media, LLC
Book Editor: Tanya T. Warren

Printed in the United States of America

LIBRARY OF CONGRESS CATALOGING-IN PUBLICATION DATA
Has been applied for.

ISBN 978-1-7031-5546-4

DEDICATION

I dedicate this book to my beloveds
who succeeded me in death:

My Husband
Joseph Haskins
1914 - 1984

My Son
Terrence A. Reed Sr.
1948 - 2011

My Grandson
James D. Reed
1972 - 2003

My Granddaughter
Shea C. Harmon
1979 - 2009

CONTENTS

ACKNOWLEDGMENTS

To my children; Tomi (Robert), Terrence (Christine), Teresa, Theda (Paul), Trudy (West), my grandchildren, my great-grandchildren, my great-great-grandchildren, my nieces, great-nieces and nephews, great-great nieces and nephews and to all those that call me Mom; you are my life long inspiration.

INTRODUCTION

For years my grands, great-grands and great-great grands often questioned me about my past — one of them even asked if I were the first woman to be born. To add, just about all fifty-nine of them have asked me how was life living in the olden days, and when was I going to write a book about my life. During the late 80's while I was living with my daughter Tomi in a suburban area of New Jersey, I saw several full moons. This brought back memories of my father (affectionately known as Papa) who always told me if I didn't tell the truth, the full moon would tell on me. Seemingly, to this day the mere thought of a moon telling on me is quite frightening. While staring at the last full moon, I reflected on my past; losing my mother at the age of two I missed her immensely. Raised by Papa who was a stern Christian full of wisdom and the best craftsman I had the pleasure of knowing, it was at that moment I decided it was time to write a book and testify about some of my life's journey and how "I Never Walked Alone" because God was always with me. The first scripture Papa taught me at the age of four was:

"Trust in the LORD with all thine heart; and lean not unto thine own understanding. ⁶ In all thy ways acknowledge him, and he shall direct thy paths." Proverbs 3:5-6.

I did not understand the scripture, he explained it to me in great detail. Now, I share with my children and grands that same scripture.

Knowing the Lord is my refuge and strong hold, I lean and put my trust in Him. He has not forsaken me yet. Ninety-three years to be exact.

THE MOON

I watched the changes of the moon
As it would wax and wane,
Sometimes I'd be so frightened,
Wondering if my life would change.
Dad said the man in the moon,
Knew my friends and even my name.
He knew if you were good or bad,
And would tell on you when it changed.
The full moon's face would look so scary,
And the last time Dad called me near,
He smilingly said,
"Try to be really good.
So the moon you won't fear.

CHAPTER ONE

In 1926, I was born in an area of Jackson, Mississippi called Georgetown. My parents were George Kelley and Iona Evans-Kelley. According to friends and family members, they were a lovely couple. I was told that my mother was one of the most gorgeous women in Jackson, being raised on a farm with her parents and five siblings full of southern charm. My father, whom we affectionately called Papa, was a successful handsome man from Greenville, Alabama that made a name for himself as a shoemaker.

As a small child I remember living in a large beautiful home on Pascagoula street in Jackson, Mississippi.

My mother, gave birth to seven children, three died in infancy – her first born was Jennie Lee, and many said she was my mother's twin, just a few years older than George, her second child; Olivia was just three years my senior and it just so happened that all of them witnessed my mother's death as she gave birth to our brother Ollie. Jennie Lee, around twelve years old, George, was ten, Olivia was five and I was two years old. Ollie lived four days and then he passed away. He was buried with my mother, in her arms. I was the only one who knew nothing of my mother.

Papa later married Ida Ransom. She had a son from a previous marriage and his name was Walter. We were a blended family of seven.

Every Sunday Papa always cooked breakfast – Hot, homemade buttered biscuits, rice, grits or fried potatoes, but always a steak; thin sliced, thick sliced it didn't matter. Papa always cooked steak. I never cared for it too much and 'til this day, I do not care for steaks. Each Sunday morning, he lectured us all while sitting at the table. We had to recite and memorize bible verses. Papa was very active in the church; we were a reflection of him. He knew the Word, stood on the Word and he wanted the same for us. Attending church and having a relationship with God was a must. He instilled in us the importance of relying on God and using wisdom. Those Sunday morning steak breakfasts fed our bellies and the Word of God fed our souls. This is when I learned Proverbs 3:5-6. To this day, it still resonates in my spirit.

This poem is dedicated to the late
George A. Kelley, Sr., my Papa.

SUNDAY SCHOOL

Thinking back many years ago of my two sisters
and brother.
Papa daily instilled in us, to always love one another.

My mother died when I was two,
the cuddling I never knew.
Papa showed love in all he did, even the spankings too.

As the Sundays came weekly, much preparation was due,
baths took place on Saturday nights,
your clothes were ready too.

Sunday mornings, we dressed quickly,
and at the table we sat.
Thanking and praising God-Oh the manners,
we couldn't forget!

So often my mouth began to water, just for a piece of
bread. Oops we could not touch one thing —until the
blessing was said.

Papa shared many scriptures —and wisdom he'd unfold.
His prayers were always long and often the bread got cold.
And then off to Sunday School, what joy that would bring.

I learned so much about the Savior and many songs I
learned to sing.

We went to church every Sunday which
was my father's rule.
He also found joy in teaching – there in the Sunday School.

Papa set a pattern for me, in acquiring a Christian tool, by
starting my Sundays off – in going to Sunday School.

CHAPTER TWO

To ease the burden on my step-mother, Jennie Lee and George were sent to the now famous Piney Woods Country Life School, just under an hour outside Jackson, Mississippi. They would come home once or twice a month. Jennie Lee was a talented musician and dancer, and George was very good for getting in to trouble. Once he set fire to the feet of a young fellow that was sleeping. He said they were stinking. He too was a musician. His instrument of choice was the trumpet.

My step mother had her hands full with Walter, Olivia and myself. Walter had polio and required a lot of attention. She wasn't the nurturing type. I can't recall too many hugs or being told I love you. Papa on the other hand gave us lots of love.

Life was exciting on Pascagoula Street in Jackson, Mississippi. I really thought I was the smartest in our family.

When asked where did I live, I'd reply "816 West P-A-S-C-A-G-O-U-L-A Street, J-A-C-K-S-O-N, M-I-S-S-I-S-S-I-P-P-I" spelling out the name of my street, city and state. Keep in mind I was only four years old. It was always a delight for me to watch Papa walk through the door from work, I would run to the back bedroom to let him in from the garage. He was always very happy to see me. I really believed life was good. Time soon changed.

During the Great Depression I can remember my step-mother putting Olivia, Walter and I in the soup line. When we gave our names we were removed from the line, because Papa was very well known around the town. Today they have social media, when I was growing up, we had "word of mouth" and that was the media. Papa's income was $19 a week. He was a highly recommended shoemaker for Jackson Shoe Hospital. He repaired shoes for the mayor, senators, and politicians from near and far. Even though everyone was affected by the Depression, those that were poor were served first. Most often it was very little to nothing left to give anyone else. Now, that I look back over my life and on Papa's endeavors and accomplishments; he was a very smart man. He was a leather salesman, ran a drycleaners, made shoes for polio patients, a carpenter, plumber, a brick layer and an electrician – and even a great speaker having only finished the 5th grade. He too "Never Walked Alone."

Due to the strain on our finances during the Great Depression, Papa decided to sell our home and move to Tougaloo, a country town a little under ten miles outside Jackson. By this time, I had learned many Psalms and scriptures. I could recite them when asked. I applied them to my life daily while adjusting in Tougaloo. Living there was a nightmare for me.

"I have been young, and now am old; yet have I not seen the righteous forsaken, nor his seed begging bread." Proverbs 37:25 KJV

We had lived in an eight room house that had electricity, gas heat, running water and a bathtub. The house in Tougaloo was a two-bedroom house that had no electricity, no gas, no running water and to top all of this we had an outside toilet (slop jars for inside use). We walked a quarter of a mile for water, and caught rain off the roof in a barrel for washing clothes and taking baths.

I don't remember how we slept in such a small house;

we did and made the best of it. We were really in a rural area, strictly country. We walked almost three miles to school. Black people walked, the white children rode buses calling us names as they passed by. It did hurt!

Papa continued to work in Jackson and Jennie Lee and George were still off at school. It was up to Olivia, Walter and I to handle the upkeep of the land, and there was plenty of it. When Jennie Lee and George did come home, they weren't much help. George took that time to play boss more than tend to chores. We had pigs in Jackson and when we moved to Tougaloo, Papa got more pigs and a cow. George would let the pigs out and have us catch the pigs. We did catch them all before Papa got home. Once, George made Walter and I wings like Cyrus Green and the Flying Machine. Walter having polio, George had to make his wings over and over again. We'd fly from the porch roof to the ground never landing quite right. I made it the second time around. We refused to fly again. Our legs were so sore. That was the type of joy George gave whenever he came home. We refused doing many of his tricks.

I had a dog named Joe B. George would use Joe B to charm snakes, then he had me put pins in their mouths and I would drag them along the ground. Telling jokes all through the day, George gave us enough laughs to last until we saw him again. He made living in Tougaloo a lot of fun after all.

This poem is dedicated to my brother, the late
George A. Kelley, Jr.

BROTHER ALWAYS CHEERED ME

I had a very pretty dog my brother called him Joe B.
Many tales he told about my dog – It all seemed a
mystery.

He said my dog had a tuxedo and florsheim boots to
match. He said Joe B dated so many dogs and was often
hard to catch.

George said the dog even had religion-'Twas to preach
one Sunday morn. He also sang in one of the choirs and
played his big bass horn.

I was only five or six when I heard this from my brother,
this was his way of cheering me up, when he knew I
missed my mother.

CHAPTER THREE

We stayed in this area of Tougaloo a year or so then moved to a larger house on Highway 51, and lived there for several years. Later, Papa purchased land near Tougaloo College's campus. He built an eight room house all by himself. It looked a lot like our house, in Jackson, except we had a lot more land, a garden and several areas for planting corn, peas and potatoes, a huge pigpen for pigs and an acre for the cow to roam.

Our cow's name was Bessie who followed and obeyed me better than anyone in our family – her care became my job. I had to feed her, water her at a pond near our house, milk her and then later churn the milk, when it became clabber. Several times I tied Bessie near the pond and ran down to a store on Highway 51 in Tougaloo. It was my sister and husband's store. The young people would meet there, dance and have fun. Of course Papa wouldn't be pleased when I came home late, so when he asked what took me so long, I lied and said the cow had run away. That never lasted because I was reminded about that full moon, so I confessed to Papa what really happened. Bravely I shared my dislike for all my chores. I told Papa I was moving to Russia, for an easier and happier life. My first poem I let Papa read, he just smiled and said, "Please send for me." He showed no remorse.

My first poem

GOING TO RUSSIA

Someday I'm going to Russia,
I won't have to churn anymore.
I won't have to wash the dishes,
not even mop the floor.
Yes, I'll go to Russia,
A place so far away.
No more hard work for me,
I'll be happy every day!

Many years later I wrote this poem...

I STAYED IN THE U.S.A.

I did not go to Russia.
I stayed in the USA.
I've had many ups and downs but made it anyway.
I made it with my family, they made my life a joy.
The equation of my life, four girls plus an only boy!

I can remember how I tried to be obedient from Papa's teaching. When we were living on Highway 51, Papa scolded Olivia and me about arguing so much. At the age of 11, I was jealous of my sister, three years my senior- her complexion, grade of hair, her popularity and brilliancy in learning. On Saturdays we had to wash our clothes – she scrubbed them and I rinsed. She would always stop washing and share with me that one day she was going to Hollywood to play in the movies. She would recite the poem "Young Lochinvar" and other poems. I was impressed but was tired of her selected poems and gestures.

One-night Papa heard us fussing over the covers on the bed. The next morning, we were told to get six strong switches – three apiece, and for both of us to give him one. He made us whip each other, and the one who was beaten, would get a whipping from him. I thought my sister was too good for him to whip.

I felt victorious when I won. Then he lashed her twice, and before he could give her the third lick, I jumped in and took the whipping for her. I begged him don't hit her anymore. He asked why, and I said, "I love my sister." From that day forward we never argued again. I share this memory in a poem.

SIX STRONG STITCHES

My sister and I always argued, while doing our chores each
day, my father got so tired of us–bit back
what he had to say.
Again he heard us squabbling and slowly
walked in the room,
I could tell he was very angry-he slammed
the floor with our new broom.

We tried so hard to be quiet, but he called us to his side,
Asking should he give us a licking,
or let us go at each other's hide.

After he had talked to us, he thought the spats were over.
As we settled down to Bed-We started
fussing over the cover.

He said "each of you get three strong Switches-Then each
of you give me one. I want you to whip each other,
I'll tell you who has won."

I knew the victory would be mine,
I whipped my sister good,
She cried and stopped hitting me – She'd
done all that she could.

The loser got the punishment, a licking from my dad,
I realized then how we had acted – we
truly made him sad.

I cried each time he hit her saying "Papa please let her go."

I learned the lesson he was teaching
don't argue anymore.
The lessons behind the six strong switches – Holds fast in
my heart today.
We never fussed anymore but loved each other dearly – 'til
she passed away.

In years to come our closeness was so bonded, I praised my sister to the point my children thought Oliva was perfect. I can truly say my Papa helped me to get rid of the jealousy. He also taught me not to worry about what others would say about me. One day his question to me, "Baby Doll if someone asked you to kiss their butt, would you do it?" I shared with him, he shouldn't say those words to me – he said "I know but, I'm still trying to prepare you for life, God does not hold you accountable for what someone says to or about you- he holds you accountable for your response." This helps me in my daily living today.

It's easy for me to forgive. From the age of four, I can remember all these things being instilled in me also in these later years.

CHAPTER FOUR

For many years, Papa would take us to see our mother's family and his family. My mother's family lived in Bond, Shadeville and Wiggins, Mississippi – his family lived in Bond, as well, also Mobile, Greenville and Selma, Alabama. It was such a joy to visit family. I can remember visiting my maternal grandfather Jack Evans, whom we affectionately called Papa Jack, an independent farmer that had acres of vegetables and fruits on his land. Sugar and flour were the only staples he purchased. He was a man of principles and integrity. My mother was his first born. Papa Jack looked a lot like a Mexican to me, you can definitely tell he was not all black.

While visiting Papa Jack, this white fellow would come to his house and they would ride their horses over his land. During this time, it was very uncommon to see a white person and anyone of color together, especially as friends. I had studied something about slavery, I questioned my grandfather – so did Olivia, asking "Are you a slave and is that man your old slave master?" Grandfather said "You'll find out one day," and I did. That fellow's name was Press Bond Jr., he was Papa Jack's half-brother, eight years his minor. They were best of friends. So much he wept over the casket, when Papa Jack died in 1962.

My great-niece wrote a report for a school project about her grandmother, my sister Olivia. My great-niece had researched and questioned relatives, and many sources, about her grandmother's grandfather, Papa Jack. My sister Jennie Lee, told many family members, the story of my Papa Jack's mother, Hulda. Her research confirmed it all to be true. Hulda, was from North Carolina and walked to Mississippi alongside Preston Bond and his brother's wagons. The slaves walked and the family was in the wagon. Upon arrival, his brothers returned to North Carolina, while Preston stayed, building the first settlement. He built a home for his wife and family. He gave Hulda land for her children when he freed them, well over five years after slavery was abolished. Hulda stayed on her land, and continued working for the Bond family.

When I read my great-niece's report, it was the missing piece to my history I had wondered about that for many years. In all the stories about slavery that Papa Jack shared with us growing up, he never mentioned anything about his real father. All along, the "Massa" he spoke of was his father, my mother's grandfather and our great-grandfather. One of the plays I wrote, "Hester's Burdened Heart" is inspired by a story Papa Jack told me as a kid.

Later in life, I walked with Dr. George Washington Carver, Marian Anderson, Lena Horne, Mary McLeod Bethune and many more prominent black celebrities while attending Tougaloo High School. Marian Anderson personally encouraged me to continue to write about black history —with the stories Papa Jack told.

Papa Jack Evans

The following is a partial list of Black History Christian plays I've written for schools, churches, non-profit groups, and a government agency.

1. *Up from Slavery*
2. *Possum Hollow*
3. *Moses*
4. *Hallelujah Ms. Daisy*
5. *Let My People Go*
6. *Coming up from Slavery*
7. *We Shall Overcome*
8. *A Dream to be Free*
9. *Jeremiah the Dreamer*
10. *Trouble in Possum Hollow*
11. *He is Risen*
12. *God is Not Dead*
13. *He Lives*
14. *Our God Resigns*
15. *Of Thee I Sing*
16. *The Birthday of a King*
17. *The Birthday of King Jesus*
18. *A Silent Night*
19. *A Love Story*
20. *Holy Night*

According to Kelly family oral history, my paternal grandfather, Dave Kelly was born a slave in Virginia, but was then sold to the Crenshaw plantation in Butler County, Alabama. Dave Kelley often related to his family, their history and his memories of Emancipation. Although a very small child, he remembered this time of a new found freedom as joyful and exciting. After slavery, Dave's father took the surname Kelley after his former "owners" in Virginia. Dave's uncle took the name of their last "owners" Crenshaw. The descendants of both brothers still inhabit the region of West Alabama. According to records, the

Reverend Dave Kelley and Jennie Cook (also born in slavery) were married in 1882. On February 4, 1891, George Asbury Kelley was born to their union in Butler County, Alabama. It was very important to me that my children knew their heritage growing up, so our vacations would consist of traveling from Pennsylvania to Alabama to Mississippi, to visit both sides of my family.

Maternal Side
Jack and Angelina Evans had:
Iona (my mother), Viola, Edmona, Homer, Agnes, Raney, Lacey, Kearney and Robert

Paternal Side
Dave and Jennie (Cook) Kelley had:
George (my father), Helen, Perlie, Annie, Lucy, Elmira, Morris, Harry, Dave and Ollie.

<u>The Kelley Family</u>
Top Left to Right
Papa (George Sr.), Mama (Iona)
Jennie Lee, George Jr.
Olivia and Thelma (me)

CHAPTER FIVE

Life near Tougaloo College seemed to bring us back to civilization. I had the privilege of escorting black celebrities on the campus as a high school honor student. As an accelerated student, I was able to enter college early. During my 11th grade year I met this fellow from Gary, Indiana, named Thomas. He was athletic and had all the moves to win games on the field. That year a "no mingling" rule was established due to the college students and high school students dating.

Between Papa's strict "no dating" rules and the school's "no mingling" rules, Thomas and I decided to go to Jackson and get married so that we could be together.

Things took a turn for the worse early on. He was drafted to serve in WWII, his emotions were all over the place, I assumed it was fear due to the war. Pearl Harbor had been attacked some years prior and the drafting law was put in place. Men had to go to war, even if they didn't want to. Many men were dying in the war, more were being drafted to take their place. Before reporting to Gary, Indiana, he forced himself on me after we had an argument. It wasn't fear. It wasn't the war. It was him.

Not long after moving to Gary, Indiana I found out I was pregnant with my oldest daughter, Tomi.

While Thomas was in training, I was feeling homesick and desired some pecans. I left our apartment and started to cross the street in the complete dark, to my scare I stepped on what appeared to be a corpse in the street – I ran back into the apartment. I prayed and prayed and quoted scriptures. I was frightened, being in a town so far from home, family and friends to a town knowing no one. I felt really homesick. I found myself wondering if it was a sign from God that I needed to head home to Mississippi. I needed the prayer life I once had before getting married.

When Thomas wrote me that he was in Fort Dix, NJ hoping all was well, I wanted to write back letting him know I was leaving Gary, Indiana and heading home. But, I didn't, I decided to stay. I did not see him again until after the birth of my daughter Tomi. He was transferred from South Carolina to the Fort Dix base in New Jersey.

While Thomas was home, it was impossible to make him happy, nothing would work and I tried endlessly to instill a peaceful environment. At that time, I did not know that this anger was caused by a condition called Olivopontocerebellar atrophy which is a form of Ataxia that starts in the brain. Not only did it affect him, but also years later it affected our children. My son died of this disease at the age of 62.

I knew this was a fight for the Lord and not me. When Tomi was six weeks old I went back home to Tougaloo. I had saved up enough money to take the train. On the train, it was announced via the intercom, that President Delano Roosevelt died, and to make matters worse, we were traveling through a flooded town. I could see water along the river almost up to the window of the train. I quickly remembered…

The LORD is nigh unto all them that call upon him, to all that call upon him in truth.[19] He will fulfil the desire of them that fear him: he also will hear their cry, and will save them.
Psalm 145:18-19 (KJV)

God was with me. I felt in my spirit He was saying "Don't

worry Thelma." I quietly prayed for Mrs. Roosevelt on the train that day. I had previously met her at the same time I met Mary McLoud-Bethune on a trip in Jackson, MS.

When I arrived home, Papa asked very few questions. He knew I was okay and he was thrilled to meet his second grand-daughter. I returned to school shortly after getting back home at a later date.

Thomas returned to college, in Tougaloo not too long after I got settled at Papa's. Life on the same campus was a disaster. Jealousy, arguing and the demons he was fighting, escalated his emotions to anger and rage. His love for music enabled him to play like a saint. In those moments he captured me. In between the captured moments and the horrible fights, I gave birth to our babies.

Three years after Tomi was born, Terrence was born; fourteen months later Teresa was born; thirteen months later, Theda was born and twenty-four months and one-day after Theda, Trudy was born.

Papa wasn't fond of Thomas at all because of his actions and angry rages. He loved his grandbabies, and went out of his way to do whatever he could for us, but Thomas he wanted little to do with. He expressed to me that he never wanted me to marry him. When Thomas and I got our own place, I stayed as long as I did because I thought I could change him. I thought the family we created was enough. The unconditional love, the stability, and compassion I provided, I thought it was all enough, it wasn't even close. This poem is to all my children, their children, and their children, and any young woman who needs these words of wisdom.

CHOOSE GOD'S MAN

We stood there watching the fellows, as they practiced
on the football field.
To our own amazement – the new fellow –caught the
ball with such awe and zeal.

Our inquiry was "who is he?"
Who's running with such a gait?
We all were interested and found out – he was the boy
from out of state.

Again we gathered at the football field,
As he ran I said he's my guy,
He soon became my boyfriend,
often times I wondered, Why?

Not only did he become my boyfriend he became my
husband 'tis true.

Five beautiful children he gave me — and many
heartaches too.

A man I said "for better or for worse,"
I had no idea it meant that every day,
I would feel cursed.

I sacrificed soo much for the sake of love,
to a man that had no idea what the meaning really was.

The more I gave the more he took,
until I had nothing left — and
he jolted- finally off the hook.

I learned from this, to wait on God
Seek His guidance in every plan.
The person you want for your mate- may
not be God's chosen man.

CHAPTER SIX

When my youngest was eight months old, Thomas left me with five children. It was no more Thomas, Thelma, Tomi, Terry, Teresa, Theda and Trudy living in Tougaloo, a riddle we'd often sing. The seven T's split. I found out that he had a child by another woman. I knew I deserved better, my children deserved better and with my mind stayed on the Lord, that it would all be better. I had perfect peace, knowing I'd never walk alone. Relying on the Lord, holding onto HIS unchanging hand, as He equipped me with grace and mercy.

Knowing Jennie Lee lived in Wichita, Kansas, and had always told me that she had promised our mother on her death bed that she'd always care for me, in pursuit of happiness, I sold my furniture and went to Wichita, Kansas.

My luggage needed a lock. Olivia's husband was to take us to the train station, but went to get a lock first – he didn't want us to leave so he purposely never came back with the lock. With or without the lock, I was determined to board that train. As we attempted to board the train the luggage opened up, and all of our clothes fell out. The conductor held the train up. He helped me gather my things and get us seated. As we were seated, the conductor found a rope and tied up the luggage, "Ain't God good!!!" We switched trains in Northern Mississippi. It was dark and eerie there while in the dimly lit waiting room. Teresa and Terry asked me to put on their pajamas (pajamas they didn't have) they were so loud they got the conductor's attention. He walked over to me and said "you know, you sho' got some pretty little darkeys." I didn't respond – yet he quickly helped me board the next train; repeating "ya'll some good looking darkeys." Between the children being restless, whining about their wishes, embracing my new fate as a single mother of five and the conductor calling my children darkey's, my patience grew slim. I whispered to God as I was looking out the window "I know you see me, I know you care, I know your grace is sufficient and I know you are here holding my hand. I surrender all." I confessed that I will not harbor anger. I knew I was not walking alone.

Upon arriving in Memphis, I could not believe it – across from the train station I saw Thomas. I knew he was going to Memphis to sign up with the federation of musicians, I just didn't think I would see him. The hotel where the federation was staying wasn't far off from where we were. I hid myself and the children so they wouldn't see him. After getting the kids their breakfast, cleaning them up from the long ride, I decided to call him and share with him a piece of my mind. I had mixed emotions - I phoned him at the hotel and said that I was taking the kids out West – he said West where? I said "maybe West hell – goodbye, I'm gone." That really wasn't my nature – but comforting words at the time. There were many soldiers there and they kept asking to help with my children and belongings, compliments on my beauty soon followed. I thought to myself, absolutely not! I just wanted to get to Wichita. I knew God had not forsaken me. I always whispered a prayer. Even to this day. "In sorrow, the name of Jesus brings joy, unspeakable joy."

Upon arriving in Wichita, Kansas, I left the children with Tomi who was nine years old at the time, and asked a lady who I met on the train to watch them at the train station.

I took a cab to my sister Jennie Lee's apartment on Water Street.

Being a country girl, I did not know I was to open the door and go inside and up the stairs to the apartments; instead, I knocked and knocked on the downstairs door; no one answered so I went back to the train station hurt and disappointed, thinking "Did I get all the way here and she left? She knew when to expect me." I was crushed, I left wondering, am I walking alone?

After an hour had passed at the station, I saw a minister (his collar gave him away) and explained my plight. He asked me to wait until he picked up his last load of people, he was transporting them to one of his conventions. He said he would take us to one of his member's home and they would try to help locate my sister. I was relieved. He kept his word by coming back. He took us to his member's house.

Once I told the member my sister's name, she said "Really! I know, Jennie Lee, she's my brother's girlfriend — and she had just had him arrested." Imagine my expression. I told her I was sorry. She said there was no need for apologies they weren't married – he was wrong for aggravating her. We stayed at her place for a while and her other brother, took us to Jennie Lee's apartment. I knocked on the door again, still no answer. He got out the car and explained I needed to go inside the building – up the stairs and knock on the door to her apartment, and not the building's front door. I laughed on the inside. Today I'm still a little country. Jennie Lee welcomed us with opened arms. She had a beautiful and fancy apartment; simply beautiful.

It didn't take us long to get settled in and I found a job at the Salvation Army. The kids and I made friends quickly and we were content and happy. Our time there was filled with good memories.

One day while in Wichita, my children and I were riding with a friend where we witnessed the Ku Klux Klan in their white garbs riding horses near our car. My friend shared with my children they were dressed up in white robes for Trick or Treat so they wouldn't be afraid. They didn't realize this was in August and not October. Another moment that God was with us. I wasn't afraid and I immediately quoted them the 23rd Psalm. Now they know all about the Klan.

CHAPTER SEVEN

During the year of 1951, my brother George moved to Wichita from Chicago. This is where he was murdered. Jennie Lee left Chester and went to Wichita, to identify my brother's body, she stayed for court and settled all of his businesses. She later got a job and made Wichita her residence for a while. This was about the time I had arrived. In October of 1952, her husband drove to Wichita for her to return to Chester. She wanted us to come with her.

We got to Chester the day Theda turned three and the next day Trudy turned one. I was in Chester nine days and began working as a dental assistant at Dr. Saltz office. I was able to get an elderly lady named Ms. Katie to care for my children. Two were in school and three were home with her. She took joy in caring for them. She took pride in washing their clothes, hanging them on the line, and ironing them. She would only accept $2.50 a week; she was a blessing. It so happened the lady who lived in the upstairs apartment where we lived, worked at the same dental office. Her brother, Guy (his actual name), would come to see her and marveled at the way I cared for my children. He pursued me – later asked me to marry him. I was not interested but when he told me he was wounded in the war and couldn't have kids that sparked my attention. He also said having had five babies, I had been loved enough. He said "I can offer you a big home, think about it." Jennie Lee made pretty compelling points as well, it felt like the right move to make. I still needed the time to think it over.

A year or two had passed by and he said he still wanted to marry me, and suggested we marry before the week was over. I told him okay, hesitantly The day we got married he had gambled all through the night to the early morning hours. His nephew had to wake him up. He wore his nephew's suit and borrowed shoes. He lost all his money that night. That should have been the sign that I was not to marry him. Again, I did not choose God's man. He was an odd character to say the least. He chided his sister for praying for him to stop gambling. I was blessed to have had a very good job. Several years later we bought a 4-bedroom home so that Terry, could have his own room. Our home was known as "the palace" and the neighborhood playground and referred to as "612" by my children's friends. I did my best to mother my children, using Papa's love as my blueprint, since I had lost my mother so young. Early mornings I would wake them up, playing many of the old songs Papa liked on our piano. As children he woke us up filing his saws and singing old songs – mostly "Jesus Keep Me Near the Cross." Those were happy moments. My children still remember the old hymns – singing them from time to time.

As time passed, Guy's habitual gambling got worse. The living conditions weren't healthy; and most times I wouldn't see him for days on end. It all had become way too much and ultimately tore our relationship completely apart.

I found solace going back to church, and helping families less fortunate than ours. It was definitely a calling on my life. Papa prayed for me to get back to church. Going and being a part of church gave me great joy. I found myself helping others just like Papa. Upon him building the large house in Tougaloo, he took in boarders that were students at Tougaloo College. This was known in the community college campus and various churches.

He charged very little for room and board helped when their funds were low, he prayed for them; and introduced them to Jesus. In later years a brick with his name was placed in front of the college chapel along with others for recognition of their services to the college and community. All of this resulted in the street that he lived on being named after him (Kelley Street).

Often I thanked God, for having had a devout Christian and loving father. Many nights I thought of Papa's teachings and the impact he had on his grandchildren. Trudy shared many times, how blessed we have been knowing all Papa did to keep the family together. My late son, Terry, loved his grandfather so much, he wanted to wear his sleeping nighties just like Papa.

The children's joy was Papa's yearly visit from Mississippi to Pennsylvania to pick them up and take them back to Mississippi to spend the summer with him. This was also my vacation.

One year, they acted up so bad, he told them when they got to the house, they had to go down yonder to get some switches, that meant they were going to get a spanking! The moment they got out the car, they quickly approached him to find out where yonder was. I could tell he was tickled by the look on his face. No yonder, no switches, no spanking. Terry later said he had learned a new way to throw a ball-to chunk it. What a new vacation vocabulary word.

Oh, and one summer a possum entered the house, the kids were stunned that Papa had no fear. He beat the possum to death; to them he was so brave! He skinned it, cooked it and served it on a plate. The kids went running out the house.

Tomi still talks about Papa's mannerisms, how much she admired and respected him, more than any man in her life. She recalls a time when she took sick while staying with him her freshman year at Tougaloo College. The doctor told Papa that Tomi had pneumonia. He was so hurt, he wanted her to sleep in the living room; even though he had gas heat, he wanted a fire in the fireplace for extra heat. He watched her rest all night and kept logs burning throughout the night. The next week when she got up feeling better, he took her shopping to pick out a warm coat. He wasn't with her when she got it, because he had to run another errand a few stores away, and when he saw that it was red, he didn't like it. Papa felt that was the color women wore to the saloons. He allowed her to keep it. The fruit of the spirit was what he lived by. That was Papa!

But the fruit of the Spirit is love, joy, peace, longsuffering, gentleness, goodness, faith... Galatians 5:22 (KJV)

Seeing the need for discipline for my children, I put them in Catholic School in Chester, PA. I wanted them to have the spiritual guidance I had growing up. Tomi, my oldest, was the mothering one. She did as she was told most of the time, Terry had a really high IQ, but he was a bit rowdy at times and didn't do his best in school. Teresa and Theda were like two peas in a pod, they both were full of life, Trudy the youngest of the five often stayed up under me. I did have to punish them at times, however they all enjoyed reading, staying in, and having a good time.

When Theda was in elementary school, I was her substitute teacher. There was an occasion when she acted up when I asked all the students for their work to be turned in, she threw her paper on my desk – trying to act like some of the other students – I turned her name into the principal. They all had to write me a five-page letter of apology and they got a paddling! She remembers this episode today. I always corrected my children when they were wrong. I took their education seriously. I wanted them to do better than I did, better than Papa did, and better than his father who was a slave, did. There is freedom in education.

One thing that I experienced in the South, that I didn't expect in the North was prejudices. It happened a lot in the schools the kids attended. In grade school, Terry was called "nig**r." In response, he turned over several desks in the classroom and was expelled. When one of Theda's classmates called her "blackie" in elementary school; she pulled the girls hair – and her classmate told the teacher that Theda had pulled her hair. Theda told the Principal what the little girl said to her, and her response was, "Well you are aren't you?"

In 8th grade Tomi took a test. The nun shared with the class that if she did not call their name, they would not be able to go to high school and without high school, they wouldn't be able to take a trade, much less attend college. Tomi's name was not called but she went on to high school anyway. She actually went to an all-girls Catholic High school.

In her 11th grade year it was announced that the person with the highest score in Biology, would be featured in the Archdiocese Circular. Tomi had the highest score, but the Nun accused her of cheating. Tomi shared with me if she couldn't go to Tougaloo College, she didn't want to go to college at all. She didn't let this get her down and when she graduated from High School, she attended Tougaloo College. We trusted the Lord and He prevailed.

Teresa entered the same high school and with two other girls played hooky, one day. They were punished and had to attend detention for more than a month. Teresa shared with me how several of her white classmates were drinking on the campus and having sex and they were punished for just one week. There was no fairness.

Upon Theda entering the same high school with high honors-she was pointed out as Teresa's sister and "needed to be watched." At the end of the school year Teresa and Theda failed several subjects. They were told to go to summer school. When the summer school program was complete the principal said something was wrong; Theresa and Theda actually had A's and B's, they didn't need to attend summer school. When the Catholic School was contacted, the principal said they could return. I told them they would not be returning, and that they were already enrolled in a co-ed boarding school.

Some people inquired, "How could I afford it?" My answer, "As a southerner we would eat Hoe Cakes and Blackstrap Molasses and sit on a box to eat, just to pursue an education."

Trudy liked hanging with Teresa and they got punished more than the others. Theda got her punishments from sheltering the others. Terry did plenty. Going to court with him. I recited the 23rd Psalm in its entirety. I changed my prayer, from asking God to keep him out of trouble to asking God that whatever happens, let me live in peace. I am proud to say, they all excelled. They all grew up doing amazing things, professionally and spiritually, doing good work in their communities and in their church. They married, and their spouses became like my own, children. All my life I have tried to live this scripture, and instill it in my family.

Trust in the LORD with all thine heart; and lean not unto thine own understanding. In all thy ways acknowledge him, and he shall direct thy paths. Proverbs 3:5-6 (KJV)

My Five T's:

L-R: Teresa, Trudy, Theda, Terry   L-R: Tomi, Terry, Teresa, Theda, Trudy

L-R: Me, Trudy, Theda, Terry, Tomi, Teresa

CHAPTER EIGHT

Real love found me later in life, actually it caught me off guard, captured me and it didn't want to let me go. I was working at the dental office, and this tall, brown eyed, bald headed man was sitting in the dental chair. I had to take his X-rays. He caught my hand and said "you have a soft touch." He held my hand as I was taking the X-ray a moment, and let it go. I felt vulnerable! I excused myself for a moment, left the room and got another nurse to wait on him. As he was leaving out, he introduced himself to me. He mentioned that he worked over at the post office, and in his spare time, he cuts hair. He asked if he could have my telephone number, but I did not give it to him; I wanted to, Lord knows I did! Every butterfly in my stomach said yes. Not only was he tall, masculine build, and clean my discernment sensed peace and serenity.

That Friday, he had an appointment to return, so I

put on my best perfume and he never showed up. I was very disappointed. He later called the office to reschedule his appointment and asked to speak with me. He explained that he was recovering from the flu. Eventually, fate would have it that we were traveling the same paths, and I finally gave him my phone number. He was very active in church and so was I. We had this in common. We would be at the same church not knowing the other was there, and every time I saw him, his natural charm swept me off my feet. During one of our conversations we discussed divorces. Would you believe we both had filed for our divorce? We prayed that our being together with counseling was approved by GOD.

Joseph was a singer and I played the piano, we enjoyed creating music together. His daughter would often sing and I played the piano for her as well. Many times Joseph would take Teresa and Theda back to boarding school. It was during this time, he told the girls of his interest and concern for me. My relationship with Joseph was in constant prayer. I needed God to confirm that he was the one. One year after our divorces were final, the Lord answered our prayers and we got married. I joined his church so that we could fellowship together. Joseph was a praying man that loved the Lord. Years had gone by, but whenever he'd walk into a room, he'd still make me blush. It felt really good to be loved according to God's word.

Joseph and Me on our wedding day.

And walk in love, as Christ also hath loved us, and hath given himself for us an offering and a sacrifice to God for a sweet smelling savour. Ephesians 5:2(KJV)

MY JOSEPH

My life became complete
when I became your wife,
So many excited things we did,
added so much joy to my life.

I admired your Christian endeavors
from the day I said I do.
You made me blissful day in and day out,
I was ecstatic knowing
you were oh so happy too.

My Joseph,
Life has not been the same
since you bade this world adieu,
I can't compete with God,
it was him who needed you.

I cried many nights, days as well,
Holding on to the promises of God
My peace is evidence His word can't fail.

My memories of you will never cease,
for I look at your picture each day,
Our life together will never pass away.

The Lord heard my plea and he blessed me with a God fearing husband that enjoyed being active in the church, caring for the kids just as much as I did.

In many ways Joseph reminded me of Papa. They both were great providers for their family, amazing cooks, they both loved the Lord, both of them had a genuine desire to help others succeed and more than anything they both loved.

In Papa's last days, my sister Olivia was his caretaker. When he took ill, I took a plane home to see him, and I read and studied the entire 103rd Psalm all the way to Mississippi. When I arrived at the hospital, my niece was reading the exact same scripture, sitting next to Papa in the hospital bed. When he saw me walk into the room, he asked me to read it to him again. I held his hand as I read...

> *Bless the LORD, O my soul: and all that is within me, bless his holy name.² Bless the LORD, O my soul, and forget not all his benefits: ³ Who forgiveth all thine iniquities; who healeth all thy diseases; ⁴ Who redeemeth thy life from destruction; who crowneth thee with lovingkindness and tender mercies. Psalm 103:1-4 (KJV)*

As he rested, I felt at peace. He did more than enough on this earth for his children, grandchildren, family, friends and even the people he didn't know. His girls were going to be sure his larger than life legacy lived on.

Papa was laid to rest in December of 1980. I don't know how I would have gotten through that moment without the Lord holding my hand, and Joseph at my side.

It was important that I continued to do the work of the Lord with my children, grandchildren and in the church. Both my heavenly and natural father would be so proud.

I wrote and directed plays, organized a children's choir of eighty-eight kids called the "Buds of Promise." Their theme song was "God Gave me a Song," they also sang "You'll Never Walk Alone." My grandchildren and later my great-grandchildren joined the choir and began singing as well. Theda's daughter Fatima, sang solos at the age of six, she sang "Great is thy Faithfulness" at Papa's funeral. Teaching and raising them, has been a joy and a delight. It inspired me to open Big Bird's Day Care, when Joseph took ill.

Joseph and I were admired by many, students from the nearby college. They had interviewed me for a school paper, and while they were there Joseph made them lunch (he was a good cook). When the doors opened to my daycare, the word got out that I was caring for children and it was not long before I was at full capacity.

Scriptures of love come to me when dealing with children.

Lo, children are an heritage of the LORD: and the
fruit of the womb is his reward.
Psalm 127:3 (KJV)

"I love them that love me; and those that seek me early
shall find me." Proverbs 8:17 (KJV)

When teaching the youth, the first scripture I taught was…

"For God so loved the world, that he gave his only begotten Son,
that whosoever believeth in him should not perish,
but have everlasting life."
John 3:16 (KJV)

In 1991 my sister, Olivia had passed away, my sister Jennie Lee and brother George were gone too. My two oldest siblings never had any children. Olivia and her husband had six beautiful girls. They call and check on me often.

They are all successful, and embody Papa's traits as well. I recall a time when Papa scolded my sister and me for not completing college. I told him we did: my children's names start with the letter "T" for Tougaloo, and Olivia's six girl's names start with the letter "C" for college, so together we completed "Tougaloo College" he wasn't amused, at all! Education was important to him, having only completed 5th grade. I only wish that he had lived to see the accomplishments of all of his family. God has truly blessed each one of us.

This poem is dedicated to all my children, my adopted children and all who celebrated my 93rd birthday with me.

ALL MY CHILDREN

Tonight has been a blessing,
Thanking God for all of you.
To see the many faces,
tells you're trusted tried and true.

Through the many years I've journeyed,
holding many a little hand, walking daily with my savior
– heeding his gentle command.

Times have not always been easy,
I've questioned my God, why?
Often in the stillness of the night, he'd wipe
my eyes when I cry.

But now I'm in my nineties – I've grown in many ways.
The problems I encountered were step to brighter days.

And now to all my children, I love you so very much.
Continue to love as God does, and always keep in touch.

CHAPTER NINE

I have had just about all of my grandchildren on a daily basis; at the time they never wanted to leave. I still watch my great-grandchildren here and there, but only one at a time. I now share the stories of my daycare and teach them the same principals.

Having all of my grand-children in my life, has made getting old easy, their love and laughs are fulfilling. I asked one of my great-great-grands how did she learn so much about the Bible and she looked at me in disbelief and said "Grandmom you should know; you are the God teaching grandmother." This blessed me and encourages me to teach as I long as I can.

I have always tried to be careful with words I said to my children before the great-grands came, I had to be a bit stern with the grands. In a weak moment I thought maybe if I'd curse at them, I'd get better results. I finally found two words and I felt good; they were "dammity hell", they laughed hysterically. It finally occurred to me that my mother would never have done this. I asked God for forgiveness. Today my grands and I still laugh about it.

If you knew which one to ask, they'd tell you they knew the Lord showed me things. I knew when they weren't telling the truth; and also knew when people didn't have their best interest at heart; saving them from getting in a lot of trouble. One of them, I saved their life and they now thank me for it. Trusting in the Lord daily meant acting on what He showed me, even if they felt for a moment I wasn't the fun grand-mom.

I found a note from one of my great-grands. It's like putting money in the bank. "Gram-Gram, I stopped by to use the bathroom, get some fruit, and of course, to see you. You're always on the move. I love you. Keep setting the tone high I can't wait to follow in your steps. I kept everything just like you left it. Love your great grand-daughter." A small note on a scratch piece of paper, yet it spoke volumes on how she sees me. I learned to not be concerned with the thoughts of others, but to those whom I leave my legacy, it means everything to know their thoughts towards me.

They've asked me, why am I so happy and full of joy whenever they see me. I often respond, "because of you." Truly, it's a blessing from God and the love I have for family and friends. The care and concern I receive at all times is nothing short of amazing.

A GRANDMOTHER

Being a grandmother was fun at first,
down through the years it seemed to get worse.
These grandchildren began having children too.
Sometimes when they come I get out of view.
I'm not really serious – I love them so much,
A handshake or kiss – I just love the gentle touch.

A GREAT-GRANDMOTHER

I walked down a pathway one day,
seeking peace and tranquility.
I wasn't sad, but wondered – What has happened to me.
I never wanted the real big things – Wanted to be a good
wife and mother, these two things did
come my way – The man in my life chose another.
Now my life's changed greatly – So I often try not to
bother, but I have to pray to
God give me strength being a great grandmother.

A GREAT-GREAT GRANDMOTHER

Sixteen so far with others on the way.
Can't finish this poem until a later day,
Love these children as I grow old.
Holding them close with their love,
I will never never get cold.
They help as I look on their faces and see,
all these grands were meant for me.

CHAPTER TEN

I have been blessed so many times by the care and attention I get during my illnesses. One of my very close friends said "Well if you don't put anything in the bank you can't get anything out." God will show you how and what to do at all times. Now that I'm much older I realize the diagnosis of some of my illnesses. A young deacon shared that my body was trying to catch up with my age, ninety-three. I never thought of it that way but I'm sure he's right.

I have had many experiences, received certificates, plaques awards and many forms of recognition. I relish these accomplishments for others to see and achieve the same. Always encourage others to use the talents God has given them.

In raising a family, know that all of your children are all different. I asked the Lord for no favoritism. I soon found out, no two treated you the same – just look for love and respect. God will see you through. He stands at the door and He knows and sees all. We are all sinners saved by grace. We make mistakes and will continue. Just remember the cross. Thinking back over the years with my children, there were good days and bad days. I have learned a lot. I've cried a lot and laughed a lot. A lot of my tears were tears of joy. While a child I was told "Love Lifted Me" was my mother's favorite song. Now it's mine.

I often looked at her picture and thought, I'm not as pretty as you, but I'm claiming your ways. She was said to have been so gentle, mild and kind. So often in the stillness of the night I wondered how she would have solved some of the situations I encountered. I learned quickly…

"Not that I speak in respect of want: for I have learned, in whatsoever state I am, therewith to be content" Philippians 4:11 (KJV)

This scripture helped me a lot. Especially the part that says "I have learned, in whatsoever state I am, there with to be content." So often we get so riled up over situations God has taken care of. There was a period in my life when my husband Joseph and later my beloved grandson James died, I thought of them daily and cried. My grandson's mother

Trudy came to visit and asked for an adopted daughter of mine to come over and pray for her and her husband. She came and prayed for them and, to this day, I cannot remember the exact words she prayed, but I stopped crying about their passing. Some years later when my sweet granddaughter Shea and my dear son Terry died, the prayer was still resonating in my mind and spirit.

No more constant weeping with tears of sorrow, but understanding – just to trust God. Through the good and the bad days, I pray daily for God's grace and mercy – remembering I am never walking alone. In spite of the loss of my husband and son and two grandchildren, He is still walking with me! I can feel it!

A PRAYER I LOVE TO PRAY:

Father, in Jesus name, I thank you for the guidance and purpose you have placed on my life. Sometimes I get confused in the path you are leading me, I'll always be thankful in knowing you will not lead me astray. Thank you for my family, friends and even my foes.

⁵ Trust in the LORD with all thine heart; and lean not unto thine own understanding.⁶ In all thy ways acknowledge him, and he shall direct thy paths. Proverbs 3:5-6 (KJV)

Father, I consider you in all my ways. I will not lean to my own understanding but trust in You completely. Your love lifted me, and I'm so grateful You never allowed me to walk alone. **AMEN**.

These are some of the virtues I try to live by. Making a list of them is a reminder to apply them daily.

1. *Always give God the praise He deserves.*

2. *Worry about nothing, pray about everything. Trust GOD.*

3. *Always be grateful.*

4. *Be a good listener.*

5. *Always encourage others.*

6. *Seek God's guidance in all you do.*

7. *Don't let anger take you where you can't afford to go.*

8. *Don't compare your life or your kids to anyone.*

9. *Count your blessings, literally name them one by one.*

10. *Share your blessings with those in need.*

11. *Cling to trust-worthy friends.*

12. *Read the Bible daily.*

13. *If you must gossip let it be about the gospel.*

14. *Get your rest and keep clean.*

15. *The struggle is not yours, it's the Lord's.*

I am a writer by nature and have inspired many people to write just as I was once advised by the late Mary Anderson. Keeping my word, I have been writing ever since, even waking up during the midnight hours to early mornings writing. Writing plays helped me to feel the characters. Their challenging rules, actually made me feel like a mom to them placing myself in the scenes as their protector, provider, and deliverer. It is an absolute joy for me to write welcomes responses, and speeches for others as well. In areas where I need help – people are there for me. I can truly say "God is a good God!" Accept Him now if you have not yet done so! I'm so glad, *I Never Walked Alone.*

Writing this book has been most pleasurable for me because it has brought back so many good memories; and especially because I can leave a message for all my children and grands, as well as others, that "You don't have to walk alone." You too can get through with God's help by accepting the Lord Jesus Christ as your personal Savior. If you haven't already done so, give your life to Jesus. He has made a way for us to live with Him eternally. He'll be your Savior, your Redeemer, you Healer, your Provider and so much more! John 3:16 says *"For God so loved the world that He gave his only begotten son, that whosoever believeth on him shall not perish but have everlasting life.* Romans 3:23 says *"For all have sinned and come short of the glory of God."* I John 1:9 says *"If we confess our sins, he is faithful and just to forgive us our sins, and to cleanse us from all unrighteousness.* God has said in His word that *He will never leave you, nor forsake you; and I can truly say that He has been with me every step of the way!* I never walked alone.

THELMA'S PATHWAY OF POEMS

May these collection of poems; bless and inspire you, whatever paths in life, you may happen upon.

NURSERY RHYMES

THE CHRISTIAN MOTHER GOOSE
Has just come to town
Spreading the word of Jesus
In the Holy Bible it's found.

She practices doing good to everyone
And prays both day and night
She teaches songs of Jesus
For she knows this way is right.

She reaches songs of Jesus
For she knows this way is right.

MARY HAS LAMB
Mary has a lamb
Jesus is His name
He loves each one of us
And treats us all the same.

SWEET BO PEEP
Sweet Bo Peep didn't lose her sheep,
She knew where to look.
They were almost sleep
Learning scriptures from the Holy Book.

FAMILY POEMS

GOOD ADVICE

Swing me once
Swing me twice
Please give me some good advice.
What advice do you have for me?
Stand way back from under the tree!

WIN THE RACE

Listen my children – you must hear
Not the midnight ride of Paul Revere
But lives of slaves many years ago
When hearts did ache through their days of woe.

Slaves were tormented, wounded and hurt
Blooded, spit on-dragged through the dirt
Their broken spirits-master did not care
They lived with hope-knowing God answers prayers.

Separated from families – some lost their hair
Often left naked-with no clothes to wear
God sits high – yes and He always looks low
Keep praying my children – Slavery has to go.

Prejudices still work lurking- we see everyday
Hatred still rises-white man sees it his way.
Keep on trotting freedom road –gold your head high
Knowing God's listening and helping slavery to die.

And now for us all-there's plenty to do
Praises for our forefathers – who prayed for us too.

We must love our enemies – It's no disgrace
With love and forgiveness – we're going to win this race.

IN THE SWING
I do know now
Just why I sing
Day in, day out
As I ponder a thing.

Sometimes it's wealth
Sometimes it's health
So bear with me – to and fro
Up and down – then onward go!

My mind goes back to childhood days
Oh yes I've changed in many ways
Thank goodness my children are out the house
It's just hubby and me
Can't you see why I swing so happily!

WEATHERING THE WINTER'S BLOW
Look out the window quickly!
Snowflakes are falling down
Whirling, twirling, falling fast
As they flurry to the ground.

I always wanted lots of snow
Hoping schools would all be closed
I'll never forget the frosted cheeks
And the redness of my nose.

Very early the next day
I jumped quickly from the bed
The snow was steadily falling
So much – I became afraid.

Soon as the snow stopped falling
We built a large snowman
His nose a carrot and button eyes
A broom was placed in his hand.

Thank you dear winter
You proved yourself with snow
Gladly I added on heavier garments
To weather your winter's blow.

IT'S SPRING

The wintry cold air has gone
I feel a warm gentle breeze
Spring has made her arrival
Gone is the cold winter freeze.

The grass gets greener every day
Leaves cover the branches on trees
I'm glad that Spring is here
I can dress now as I please.

We scratch the earth in planting
Birds are singing in the air
Easter always comes in Spring
Flowers are blooming everywhere.

Spring will soon be over
Summer is on her way
Let's thank God for the seasons
Whatever the weather, let's pray!

SUMMER COMES AND ENDS

Following Spring comes summer
When we wear few clothes
We wonder what the temp will be
So changeable no one knows.

The sun gets hotter and hotter
Off to the beach we go
Splashing in the ocean waters
As the sun, blisters each toe.

We help the children build castles
Using also a pail and a spade
Soon it gets so very hot
Then run for the umbrella's shade.

Summer is so very special
Traveling to visit family and friends
Tire from the hustle and bustle
Summer has to end!

AUTUMN

I'm so glad that it is Autumn
The fields are turning brown
I enjoy walking through the orchards
Picking fruit from off the ground.

I gather many vegetables
That will be freezer packed
The cornstalks have been cut
Neatly by the barn they're stacked.

It's such a joy at harvest
With food to share with friends
Let us all thank God our father
For the harvest He did send.

THIRD GRADE AT TOUGALOO

I attended Daniel Hand School
On the grounds of Tougaloo College
It was the school of my father's choice
For his daughters to seek after knowledge.

I liked all of my teachers
I thought they were all so great
Even our principal with his accent
There never was one I could hate.

In third grade we changed classes
Different skills we had to do
Each teacher was a new experience
A change for us students too.

That year we began writing with ink

The ink well was always in view
So often my ribbons were dabbed with ink
Taking on a blueish hue.

The boy who sat behind me
Wrote me notes all during the day
Telling me how much he liked me
Gave me candy when we went to play.
The teacher sent his note to my home one day
Then I knew I was in a fix
To hear these famous words from Papa
Saying, "Child, boys and books don't mix!"

But I'll always remember that third grade
So much studying I had to do
Yes, it was the year I enjoyed the most
There at dear old Tougaloo.

THE SETTING SUN

There was a time when my eyes were swollen
I had cried so much that day
I prayed and cried unto the Lord
Why did they take my Mother away?

Down there in the dismal cornfields
You worked hard, not stopping to rest
Mama said to me so often
Follow the sun as it set in the west.

Oh the day that mama left me
She rode away with Ol' Master's wife
I thought how I never had it easy
Living a tormented miserable life.

Those words she said I remembered
One day as the sun began to set
I am now strong —don't cry anymore
To my mama I must get.

West at the bend of the river
Sun setting as darkness did hover
I ran to the river, fast as I could
There mama started crossing over!

On the other side of the river
Mamma and Papa with me met
O' the oppression of the life of a slave
I don't think I'll ever forget.

Thinking back on my life so long ago
When I kneel on my knees to pray
Thank God for the memory of the setting sun
Is what saved my life that day.

A VERY SPECIAL CHILD

One day this baby came from the hospital
The question was asked openly
Will you take care of our baby?
Mom gently passed her to me.

I said "You haven't seen my credentials
You're trusting your baby with me?
Mom and Dad responded together
Yes! for real and not maybe!"

She came to me in October
Mom sent instructions the size of a book
I grew to love her so very much
Her care, I never forsook.

This little girl sat at the piano
She always tried to sing
This was her beginning in music
As she let her laughter ring.

And now she's a young lady
I'll never forget her smile
She was so dear and precious
A very very special child.

Whether she continued her music
She made an early hit with me
I can still see her playing the piano
Singing so happily.

DADDY'S LOOK

To stay out late at night
 I knew I wasn't allowed
Thinking I had truly grown up
I tried partying with the crowd.

I came home early one morning
Yes, I knew I was in trouble
Just seeing the look in my father's face
I knew my trouble could double.

I was grounded for a month
I had lost my father's trust

No fussing no lickings he gave me
But a look of total disgust.
That was punishment enough.

LITTLE PEOPLE

Up and down the stairway
Little people did run
Sometimes getting on my nerves
They're really having fun.

Stop the Nosie immediately
I would quickly say
But then I was reminded
I was young one day.

THE BIRDS NEST

There's a tall tree in the backyard
Birds are always nesting there
They fly and swoop down at you
Protecting their nest with care.

Little birds have been hatched
Stop by and look with me
You'll see the chirping happy birds
Up in the tree.

SPIRITUAL POEMS

GOD'S UMBRELLA

There will be days when you are sad
Maybe grief, loneliness and pain.
The skies will grow dark and dreary
But the sun will shine again.

Jesus will always be with you.
The life seems hard to bear
Just pray for peace and contentment
Oh yes our savior does car.

Try to wear laughter on your lips
When the road seems not to end
My father is always with you
And the comforter He did send.

God shows His love in the sunshine
And even when it rains
We thank Him for the harvest
Of fruit and the golden grain.

I can see His many miracles
In every moment that passes by
He's truly blessed each one of us
Under the umbrella of His blue sky.

I CANNOT COUNT THEM ALL

I received and accepted the ministry
That God has given to me
To care and nurturer little ones
And treat them tenderly.

All the times they don't obey
The way I wished they would
Yet I continue to love each one
And praise them as I should.

It is not hard to visualize
When someone needs a touch
A gentle pat – a hug or kiss
Is needed so very much.

There have been many hurdles
I've had to take in stride
I always let my children know
It's in Jesus I must abide.

Now through these many many years
I know God is leading me.
No, all the faces I cannot count
Yet I rejoice, so happily.

Why should I try to count each child?
When my God knows each one-
The continuous blessings of happiness,
Is the victory I have won.

THE HOLY BOOK

Many many books I've read
Where I traveled so far away
To some the highest mountains
And even to a tranquil bay.

I've crossed many bodies of water
Thru the many books I've read
I've slept in eerie houses
So haunted, that I was scared.

I've traveled many pathways and flowers – I did pick;
I've read many stories (mysteries)
Magic with many a trick.

And then I picked up the Bible
It is God's Holy Word
From Genesis to Revelation
A message can be heard.

I recommend this Holy Book
Read it through and through
You'll learn of his truth and goodness
And now He loves me and you.

GOING TO CHURCH

Saturday nights were so sleepy
Preparing Sunday clothes to wear
Always rising early to go to church
Is something our family had to share.

I really liked singing and reading the WORD
And the messages I enjoyed so much
The many many blessings that I received
By rising early and going to church.

FAMILY

Have you ever stopped one moment
Just to think of your family?
Each is a prime component,
In making this unity.
Yes, we are all different
Possessing an individual look
But the love we radiate
Comes from reading the Holy Book.

BLACK HISTORY POEMS

A DREAM TO BE FREE

Lizzie, look into my eyes dear child
And please don't tell a lie
What is it that's bothering you?

Mama, Mary slipped me pencils and books
After I cleaned their kitchen one night,
I sneaked and hid them under my pallet
And I knew this wasn't right.

I've learned so quickly how to read and write
And I've almost finished a book,
Please don't scold me for what I did
It's learning that I forsook.

I've dreamed of days when we must go
To a place far, far away
Now that I'm learning to read and write
You'll be proud of me someday.

I could not look you in the face
Knowing the thing I had done
Won't you listen to things I've learned
To me it's been such fun!

I also have this map for you
Of the place where our lives will grow
Harriet Tubman is coming soon
With her we must surely go.

Now this is that dream of mine
And it's truly our destiny –
The time has come to go to that place
And realize we'll be free.

THEY DON'T UNDERSTAND

She sat there mediating – so all alone
Her fists were clinched so very tight
She prayed so fervently to God
Saying, "Why can't they treat us right?"

Does the color of my skin
Tell the world I'm of no worth?
My Lord gave me the answer
Now I can go forth on this earth.

Now I sing and pray for I'm happy!
And the Bible I hold in my hand.
The answer God revealed to me
Our existence they don't understand.

THE BLACK MAN'S THEATER

It was down at the old plantation
Where the black man played his role
He joked, laughed, and rattled the worn jawbones.
Seeking solace for his down-trodden soul.

He picked out special hickory sticks
To beat out his favorite tunes
Banging hard the blacksmith's rasps
Harmonizing with the beating of spoons.

This was the beginning of the black man's theater.
Not always in splendor but awe
The uniqueness and brilliancy of the black man
Is just what the white man saw.

YOUR ACCOMPLISHMENT

Thanks to our Afro-Americans
For our inventions now on hand
You helped in America's civilization
Don't stop, take your rightful stand.

To our young Afro-Americans
Many inventions are still needed
Strive hard in the field of education
Dreams of fore parents should be healed.
Young Afro-Americans be thoughtful
Continue to conquer your books
You can and must prove to the world
It's your worth and not your looks.

Use your imagination freely
There are more inventions for you.
Study hard and put your minds in gear
And please come shining through.

Trying may not be too easy
But persevere to the end
Whether an invention or patent
Your accomplishments will truly win.

MAYBELLE

Maybelle was heard crying in the cotton field
As she tried to stand up straight
She was hurting from the bloody bruises.
When she was beaten by the garden gate.

She had lost all of her children
They were taken away late one night,
She's harboring some deep dark feelings
Knowing Master never treated her right.

Jakes came with her from Africa
He left her with a bruised and bloody back
She does not know where he is
But he's hiding in the old cotton shack.

Ol' Master keeps threatening Maybelle,
saying "don't stop 'til you finish that cotton row.
Yet ol' Jake is planning their getaway
And Maybelle just don't know.

She kept on picking cotton
In her eye you could see a tear-
She had so much hate now in her heart,
The noises she could not hear.

Down at the end of that long cotton row
Jake finally crept into sight-
They slowly traveled through the cotton field, and
They vanished in the night.

TRIBUTES

MY SISTER JENNIE LEE
My sister attended boarding school
Came home every other week
My sister fascinated me so
When she came I could hardly speak.

She was oh so beautiful
Often called one of the most beautiful girls
Her complexion so soft and so peachy
And a head of black bubbly curls.

She possessed so many talents
Dancing, singing, and blowing the trombone
To me she was the fairest of many
Like a queen sitting on her throne.

A song was written about her
Saying she was so beautiful to see
This girl attending Piney Woods School
Is our own sweet Jennie Lee.

A TRIBUTE TO BETTY
Betty you were different
Unique in many ways,
Your legacy was kindness
I'll be missing through the days.

You knew sorrow from day to day
And was stung by illness too
But neither put you in despair

Nor did your faith subdue.

I knew when you heard death coming
You never cowered in fear
But cried out so loudly,
Dear Lord, I'm over here.

Friend, Forgive me for crying
Still wishing you were here –
It's hard to give up a friend
Whom you've learned to love so dear.

Because you were different and special
It was hard to face you were gone
Blessings now surround me,
Knowing you're with God in your brand new home.
I'll do my best to make your children my concern.

THEY'RE ALL GROWN
I once looked at my little ones
Counting their fingers and toes.
I even think of the many haircuts
And how I tried to do cornrows.

I'm startled now as I look at them
How the families continue to grow
Little fingers and little toes,
I can't count them anymore.

Now I've grown from Mama, to Grandma,
But the love keeps passing on.
The grands are now doing the counting,
Guess what? They too are now grown!

ABOUT THE AUTHOR

Thelma is currently a member of Providence Baptist Church, where she is a member of the Adult Sunday School, the Drama Ministry, Advisor of the Sarah Harrell Missionary Ministry and the Parent Club. She also serves as Supervisor of the Chester District Congress of Christian Education, and formerly of the Women's Aglow and the Women's Ministry of the Brotherhood Breakfast Association of Churches.

Thelma, continues to write plays and poems, through the urging of her family. At ninety-three, she continues to confess that she is truly blessed and not stressed, through the blessings of the Lord and Savior Jesus Christ.

Thelma resides in Pennsylvania and enjoys helping others, solving crossword puzzles and spending time with her four children, thirteen grands, thirty-one great-grands, sixteen great-great grandchildren.

For more about this book and author, visit:

http://bit.ly/ThelmaKHaskins

THELMA'S PATHWAY OF POEMS BOOK

COMING SOON!

Made in the USA
Lexington, KY
24 November 2019